CHILDREN'S ROOM

W9-CTC-267

Chickens

Leo Statts

abdopublishing.com

Published by Abdo Zoom™, PO Box 398166, Minneapolis, Minnesota 55439. Copyright © 2017 by Abdo Consulting Group, Inc. International copyrights reserved in all countries. No part of this book may be reproduced in any form without written permission from the publisher. Abdo Zoom™ is a trademark and logo of Abdo Consulting Group, Inc

Printed in the United States of America, North Mankato, Minnesota
092016
012017

Cover Photo: George Clerk/iStockphoto
Interior Photos: Suriya Silsaksom/iStockphoto, 1; FiledImage/iStockphoto, 4–5; iStockphoto, 7, 9, 13, 18; David Stephenson/iStockphoto, 8; Hilde Anna/Shutterstock Images, 10; Shutterstock Images, 11, 12; George Clerk/iStockphoto, 15, 17; Wiktor Rzeżuchowski/iStockphoto, 16; Nataliia Melnychuk/Shutterstock Images, 19; Red Line Editorial, 20 (left), 20 (right), 21 (left), 21 (right)

Editor: Emily Temple
Series Designer: Madeline Berger
Art Direction: Dorothy Toth

Publisher's Cataloging-in-Publication Data
Names: Statts, Leo, author.
Title: Chickens / by Leo Statts.
Description: Minneapolis, MN : Abdo Zoom, 2017. | Series: Farm animals | Includes bibliographical references and index.
Identifiers: LCCN 2016948664 | ISBN 9781680799033 (lib. bdg.) | ISBN 9781624024894 (ebook) | ISBN 9781624025457 (Read-to-me ebook)
Subjects: LCSH: Chickens--Juvenile literature.
Classification: DDC 636.5--dc23
LC record available at http://lccn.loc.gov/2016948664

Table of Contents

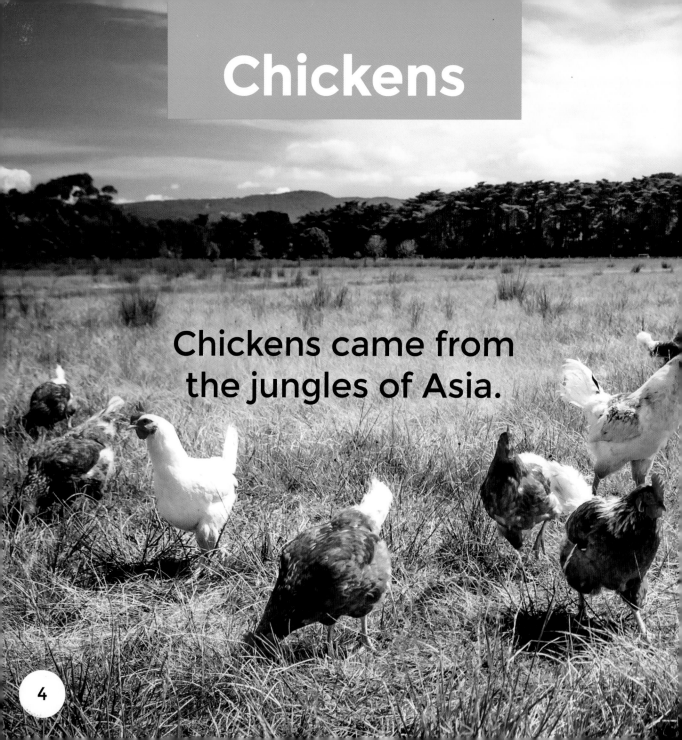

Chickens

Chickens came from the jungles of Asia.

People started keeping chickens more than 5,000 years ago. Today most chickens live on farms.

Body

Some chickens are
brown, black, or white.
Others have many colors.

Chickens have a red comb on their heads.

They also
have a red
wattle.

9

Chickens get scared easily.

They move their wings back
and forth when they are afraid.

Food

Chickens mostly eat grains.
They also eat insects.

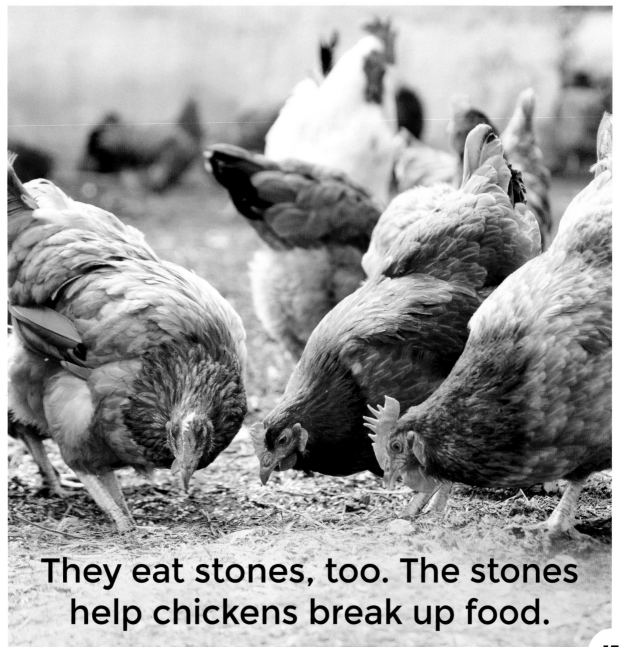

They eat stones, too. The stones help chickens break up food.

Farm Life

Some chickens are raised for their meat. They are called **poultry**. Female chickens also lay eggs for people to eat.

Many chickens live in cages.

They sometimes live in **coops**.

Names

Female chickens are called hens. Roosters are male chickens.

We call baby chickens chicks.
They **hatch** from eggs.

Average Height

A chicken is taller than a basketball.

12 in

9.5 in

Average Weight

A chicken is heavier than a textbook.

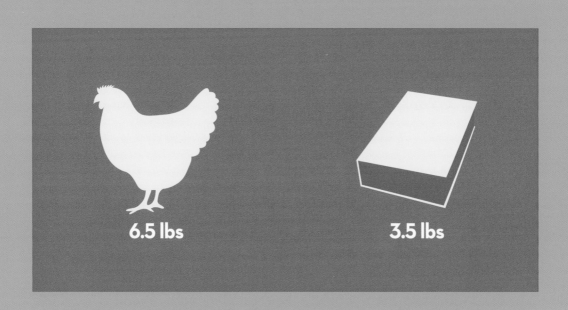

6.5 lbs

3.5 lbs

Glossary

comb - a soft part on top of the head of some birds.

coop - a small building where chickens are kept.

grain - the seeds of plants that are used for food.

hatch - to be born from an egg.

poultry - birds that farmers raise for food.

wattle - skin that hangs from the head or neck of some birds.

Booklinks

For more information
on chickens, please visit
booklinks.abdopublishing.com

Z**m In on Animals!

Learn even more with the Abdo Zoom
Animals database. Check out
abdozoom.com for more information.

Index